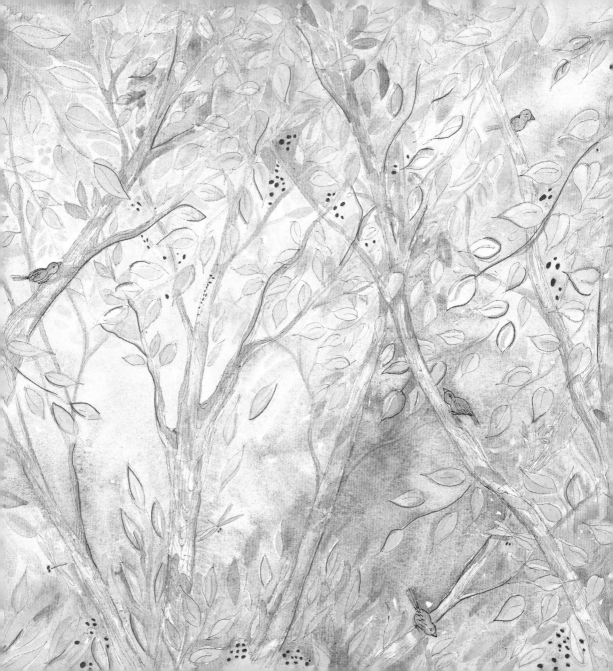

To _____

From _____

_____

Mother's Treasury

For information write Andrews McMeel Publishing,
4520 Main Street, Kansas City, Missouri 64111.

www.beckykelly.com

05 06 07 08 09 EPB 10 9 8 7 6 5 4 3 2 1

ISBN: 0-7407-5031-3

Illustrations by Becky Kelly
Design by Stephanie R. Farley
Edited by Polly Blair
Production by Elizabeth Nuelle

Mother's Treasury

illustrated by Becky Kelly

**Andrews McMeel
Publishing**

Kansas City

For my Mother.

—B.K.

Introduction

I don't think there is anything that can ever totally prepare you for motherhood.

The world of motherhood: a wonderful place where you could spend all day just watching the precious little creature who has entered your life. A world full of diapers and a carpet of toys and socks so tiny that you smile every time you wash them.

A mother knows she would go to the ends of the Earth for her child—do anything they need, be there for every scrape and tear. A mother also knows that her child needs room to grow into the wonderful person she knows they will become. At some point a mother has to trust that she has given her child the roots they need to live, and then stand back and watch her child grow their own beautiful, strong branches and lustrous leaves as they stretch toward the sun to become an adult.

No one can portray the wonder of a new baby or the innocence of childhood quite like artist Becky Kelly. Her paintbrush manages to capture the perfect curve of a baby's plump cheek and the exuberance of a child at play. This *Treasury* is a collection of Becky's sumptuous illustrations and some of her favorite poems, stories, and sayings. I invite you to dive into these beautiful pages to laugh at a special story that might remind you of when your child was young, or to linger over a poignant poem, or be touched by the beauty of Becky's art as she celebrates that most noblest of professions: motherhood.

—Polly Blair, Editor

A mother is she
who can take the place
of all others
but whose place
no one else can take.

—Cardinal Mermillod

By no amount of agile exercising of a wistful imagination could my mother have been called lenient. Generous she was; indulgent, never. Kind, yes; permissive, never. In her world, people she accepted paddled their own canoes, pulled their own weight, put their own shoulders to their own plows and pushed like hell.

—Maya Angelou

I shall never forget my mother,

for it was she who planted and nurtured

the first seeds of good within me.

She opened my heart to the impressions of nature;

she awakened my understanding

and extended my horizon,

and her precepts exerted an everlasting influence

upon the course of my life.

—Immanuel Kant

You never get over bein' a child
long's you have a mother to go to.

—Sarah Orne Jewett

To a mother, children are like ideas;
none are as wonderful as her own.

—Chinese Proverb

The heart of a mother is a deep abyss at the bottom of
which you will always discover forgiveness.

—Honoré de Balzac

A Sweet Treat for Mom
Glazed Almonds

Ingredients

1 cup whole blanched almonds

1/2 cup sugar

2 tablespoons butter

1/2 teaspoon vanilla

Directions

In an iron skillet, combine whole almonds, sugar, and butter. Cook, stirring constantly, over medium-low heat until almonds are well-coated and the sugar is golden brown (about 15 minutes).

Stir in vanilla. Spread nuts on a large sheet of aluminum foil. Working quickly with two forks, immediately separate the almonds. Sprinkle the glazed nuts lightly with salt; let cool.

Present to Mom in a small container with a bright bow.

Memories of Mama

Holding hands crossing streets.

Crayons, markers, colored pencils, glue.

Button eyes on sock puppets.

Reading aloud, reading quietly, but always together.

Long conversations deep into the night.

Crying on the laundry room floor on the phone far away.

Special food when sick.

(Pretending to be sick for extra attention.)

Playing in makeup.

Playing in the snow.

Buying new shoes.

Talks about boys and husbands, finances and futures.

Tears saying good-bye, tears coming home.

Discussing the state of the world.

Always a heartbeat away.

—Annie Mitchell

The Lark

(A Hindu Fable)

A child went up to a lark and said, "Good lark, have you any young ones?"

"Yes, child, I have," said the mother lark, "and they are very pretty ones, indeed." Then she pointed to the little birds and said, "This is Fair Wing, that is Tiny Bill, and that other is Bright Eyes."

"At home, we are three," said the child, "myself and two sisters. Mother says that we are pretty children, and she loves us."

To this the little larks replied: "Oh, yes, *our* mother is fond of us, too."

"Good mother lark," said the child, "will you let Tiny Bill go home with me and play?"

Before the mother lark could reply, Bright Eyes said: "Yes, if you will send your little sister to play with us in our nest."

"Oh, she will be so sorry to leave home," said the child, "she could not come away from our mother."

"Tiny Bill will be so sorry to leave our nest," answered Bright Eyes, "and he will not go away from *our* mother."

Then the child ran away to her mother, saying: "Ah, every one is fond of home!"

—P. V. Ramaswami Raju (adapted)

Mothers

are instinctive philosophers.

—Harriet Beecher Stowe

My mother said to me,
"If you become a soldier, you'll be a general;
if you become a monk, you'll end up as the pope."
Instead, I became a painter and wound up as Picasso.

—Pablo Picasso

One of the oldest human needs
is having someone to wonder where you are
when you don't come home at night.

—Margaret Mead

Mama was my greatest teacher,
a teacher of compassion, love and fearlessness.
If love is sweet as a flower,
then my mother is that sweet flower of love.

—Stevie Wonder

My mother drew a distinction between achievement and success. She said that "achievement is the knowledge that you have studied and worked hard and done the best that is in you. Success is being praised by others, and that's nice, too, but not as important or satisfying. Always aim for achievement and forget about success."

—Helen Hayes

Motherhood

When I first looked at baby's face
I thought I heard the angels sing,
Their music seemed to flood the air,
And in my heart it seemed to ring.

For a moment I was lifted
Far above all earthly things;
And a grateful prayer I murmured
For the joy a baby brings.

—Hilda Ford Sherman

Baby Shoes

Two worn little shoes with a hole in the toe!
And why have I saved them? Well—all mothers know
There's nothing so sweet as a baby's worn shoe
And patter of little steps following you.

The feet they once held have grown slender and strong;
Tonight they'll be tired after dancing so long . . .
I guided her feet when she wore such as these . . .
Dear God, may I ask, won't You guide them now, please?

—Isla Paschal Richardson

Mama's Lullaby

Baby dear, Mama's here,
Watching o'er your slumber.
Dream, my child, until the dawn
Wakes the daisies on the lawn.

Dream you float in a boat,
Under starry heavens;
Dreams of brooks and singing birds,
Scented breezes, tender woods.

Dream of all, great and small,

Things serene and lovely;

Fairies, lambs, and butterflies,

Sleepy clouds in summer skies.

Sleep all night, in my sight,

Though you're off in dreamland;

Then, tomorrow, with the sun,

Back to Mama, little one!

—Grace Hall
French Folk Song

Lemon Meringue Pie

I can still see Nana after every Sunday dinner
trying to divide her lemon meringue pie
into nine perfectly equal pieces.

Anticipation of its frothy sweet, slightly tart taste
hovered around our tongues like tulle on a ballerina's tutu.
And each of us dreamed of stuffing ourselves with the whole pie
instead of just our piece.

We watched every movement of the knife in her hand
as if it were a magic wand,
and sat as quietly as we could
so that she would not lose count
and have to start all over again.

"Now, let's see," she'd say. "How many of us are there . . .
one, two, three . . ." and her voice would trail off
as she drew imaginary lines on the crust.
Then suddenly, she'd smile and look up at us.
We'd hold our breath hoping she had not lost count.

Elaborately she'd hand out the first piece,
which, of course, had to be passed clear around the table.
Each of us held onto the plate as long as we could
before the next one grabbed it out of our grasp.

What we did not know then was Nana was stalling.
She did not want it to go too quickly.

She wanted us to appreciate the hours
it had taken her to make that pie for us—
her body bent at an oblique angle to the dough
as she kneaded and rolled it out.

In the background, the TV blared soaps,
as she argued with herself about the crust's thickness,
whether the egg whites were stiff enough,
the lemon jelled just right.

And the flavor? She held the delicate confection
to her lips. It melted on her tongue.
Her eyes focused on a tiny speck of linoleum
as she tried to decide: was it sweet enough
but not too sweet, perhaps, just a trace tart.

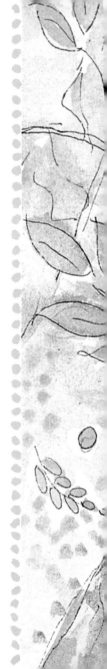

She'd pause every once in a while to listen
to a crucial piece of conversation
on *The Days of Our Lives*
so she would not lose the story line
and could discuss her suspicions.

Finally, my long-awaited piece was on the plate before me.
I wolfed down the first bite as fast as I could
By the second or third, I was lost in a cloud of meringue,
the taste heightened by a lemon so luscious it literally
caressed my tongue, and the crust full of a delicate flake
that did not crumble at the touch of a fork.

And each succeeding Sunday, I noticed,
this ritual took just a little longer.
We talked more as we lingered over that pie
like a film in slow motion.

Only now, after she is long passed,
and each of us have gone our separate ways,
do I know the only ingredient in her pie
that I ever dreamed about: the love.

—Carolyn J. Fairweather Hughes

Then came a young child whose years
Were five, but he ran and shouted:
"Love is my father, and love is my mother,
And no one knows of love but my mother
and my father."

—Kahlil Gibran

Insomniac

Bare feet padding
down a carpeted hallway
She calls me
Her tiny voice
comes to stand in the doorway
Plump fingers
pull on fat pig tails
rub widening eyes
Round belly pokes out
of cotton nightie
Toes on cold linoleum,
she considers thirst
uncloseted monsters
or watery nightmares
the best excuse
for being up this late
lips pout
she could always make me smile
so I,
hold out my arms
& she comes tumbling in.

—Esperanza Cintrón

How to Say "Mother" in Twenty Languages

Albanian—nâna	Greek—mit'ra
Arabic—el-oum	Hungarian—anya
Bulgarian—máyka	Italian—madre
Czech—matka	Latvian—mâte
Danish—moder	Norwegian—mor
Dutch—moeder	Polish—matka
Estonian—ema	Serbo-Croatian—majka
Finnish—äiti	Spanish—madre
French—mère	Swedish—moder
German—Mutter	Turkish—anne

A Poem for My Momma

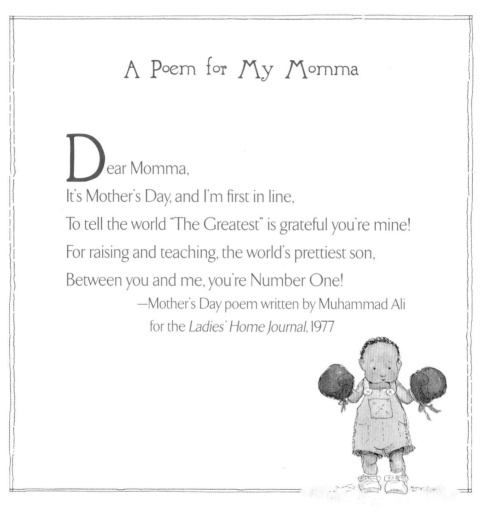

Dear Momma,
It's Mother's Day, and I'm first in line,
To tell the world "The Greatest" is grateful you're mine!
For raising and teaching, the world's prettiest son,
Between you and me, you're Number One!

—Mother's Day poem written by Muhammad Ali
for the *Ladies' Home Journal*, 1977

Romance fails us...

and so do friendships ...

but the relationship of Mother and

Child remains indelible and indestructible ...

the strongest bond upon this earth.

—Theodor Reik

A mother must precede separation
with preparation.
—Unknown

Mother's love is peace.
It need not be acquired,
it need not be deserved.
—Erich Fromm, psychologist

Mother love is the fuel
that enables a normal human being
to do the impossible.
—Unknown

A mother's sympathy
serves as an emotional Band-Aid
for a bruised ego.

—Haim G. Ginott

Education commences at the mother's knee,
and every word spoken
within the hearing of little children
tends towards the formation of character.

—Hosea Ballou

Round the idea of one's mother,
the mind of man clings with fond affection.
It is the first thought stamped in our infant hearts,
when yet soft and capable to receiving
the most profound impressions,
and all the after feelings of the world
are more or less light in comparison.
I do not know that even in our old age
we do not look back to that feeling as
the sweetest we have ever known through life.

—Charles Dickens

M is for the million things she gave me

O means only that she's growing old

T is for the tears were shed to save me

H is for her heart of purest gold

E is for her eyes, with love-light shining

R means right, and right she'll always be

Put them all together they spell "Mother,"

A word that means the world to me.

—Words by Theodore Morse
and Howard Johnson, 1915

$\mathcal{M}$otherhood is being available to your children
whenever they need you,
no matter what their age or their need.

—Major Doris Pengill

God could not be everywhere,
so He made mothers.

—Unknown

If it had not been for my mother I doubt if I could have made a success of pantomime. She was one of the greatest pantomime artists I have ever seen. She would sit for hours at a window, looking down at the people on the street and illustrating with her hands, eyes and facial expression just what was going on below. All the time, she would deliver a running fire of comment. And it was through watching and listening to her that I learned not only how to express my emotions with my hands and face, but also how to observe and study people.

It seems to me that my mother was the most splendid woman I ever knew. . . . I have met a lot of people knocking around the world since, but I have never met a more thoroughly refined woman than my mother. If I have amounted to anything, it will be due to her.

—Charles Chaplin

D on't aim to be an earthly Saint,

with eyes fixed on a star,

Just try to be the fellow

that your Mother thinks you are.

—Will S. Adkin

We must learn not to disassociate the airy flower from the earthy root, for the flower that is cut off from its root fades, and its seeds are barren, whereas the root, secure in mother earth, can produce flower after flower and bring their fruit to maturity.

—The Kabbalah

The hand that rocks the cradle
is the hand that rules the world.
—W. R. Wallace

The mother's heart is the child's schoolroom.
—Henry Ward Beecher

Parents Are People

Mommies are people
People with children.
When mommies were little
They used to be girls,
Like some of you,
And then they grew.

And now mommies are women,
Women with children,
Busy with children
And things that they do.
There are a lot of things
A lot of mommies can do.

Some mommies are ranchers
Or poetry makers
Or doctors or teachers
Or cleaners or bakers
Some mommies drive taxies
Or sing on TV
Yes, mommies can be
Almost anything they want to be.

—Carol Hall

Mother o' Mine

If I were hanged on the highest hill,
Mother o'mine, O mother o'mine!
I know whose love would follow me still,
Mother o'mine, O mother o'mine!

If I were drowned in the deepest sea,
Mother o'mine, O mother o'mine!
I know whose tears would come down to me,
Mother o'mine, O mother o'mine!

If I were damned of body and soul,
I know whose prayers would make me whole,
Mother o'mine, O mother o'mine!

—Rudyard Kipling

A Sweet Treat for Mom

Bundles of Joy

Ingredients

1 sheet frozen puff pastry

flour

1/2 cup semisweet chocolate chips

10-12 caramels, unwrapped

1/4 cup chopped walnuts

confectioners' sugar

Directions

Thaw pastry. Preheat oven to 400 degrees.

Lightly flour a flat surface. With a rolling pin, roll pastry into a 12-inch square. Lightly flour a table knife and cut pastry into four equal squares.

In the center of each square, place small handfuls of chocolate chips, caramels, and walnuts.

Bring corners of each square together; twist the ends and turn.

Place bundles twisted end up on an ungreased cookie sheet.

Bake 10 to 15 minutes or until pastry is golden.

Remove from oven and let stand for 10 minutes. Sprinkle with confectioners' sugar and serve warm.

Serves 4

Mother in Sunlight

I tugged at your skirt, and you smiled.
You stood in sunlight
Near the coal stove
A black iron heating,
A black iron slicking wrinkles
On percale dresses and starched white shirts.
You stood in sunlight
Sweat dripping down your brow.

I think of the hours you spent
To make our world sparkle.

—Louise Robinson-Boardley

Taken from

Advice for Good Little Girls

If your mother tells you to do a thing, it is wrong
to reply that you won't. It is better and more
becoming to intimate that you will do as she bids
you, and then afterwards act quietly in the matter
according to the dictates of your better judgment.

You should ever bear in mind that it is your
kind parents that you are indebted for your food,
and your nice bed, and your beautiful clothes,

and for the privilege of staying home from school when you let on that you are sick. Therefore you ought to respect their little prejudices, and humor their little whims and put up with their little foibles, until they get to crowding you too much.

Good little girls should always show marked deference for the aged. You ought never to "sass" old people—unless they "sass" you first.

—Mark Twain
June 24, 1865

The precursor of the mirror is the mother's face.

—D. W. Winnicott

The mother . . . the mysterious source
of human life, where nature
still receives the breath of God . . .

—Pope Paul VI

A mother understands what a child does not say.

—Jewish proverb

Yⁿou may have tangible wealth untold;

Caskets of jewels and coffers of gold.

Richer than I you can never be—

I had a mother who read to me.

—Gillian Strickland,
The Reading Mother

Jafta's Mother

I would like you, said Jafta, to meet my mother.
There is nobody I know quite like my mother.
My mother is like the earth—full of goodness,
warm and brown and strong. My mother is like the sun
rising in the early morning, lighting up the dark corners
and gently coaxing us awake. She prods the fire into life
and soon everywhere is filled with the smoky smell of
food, bringing rumbles to my tummy and making me
want to get up.

As the sun starts its day and the flowers burst open to turn and follow it across the sky, I think of my mother. Like the sky, she's always there. You can always look up and see her. At midday when the sun is high and strongest, she shades and comforts us, like the willows on the bank of the river. Or when the day has become too hot and stuffy, she cools us as the rain does when it turns the dust-bowls into rippling puddles, washing out the grass and making it green again.

She doesn't often complain, even in the bad times. But beware! If she finds you cheating at a game, or teasing your younger sisters, she can sound like thunder in the afternoon and her eyes will flash like the lightning out of the dark clouds.

My mother doesn't often storm, said Jafta, and it's much nicer when she sings. She sings to us as she cooks the evening meal. If you've heard a hoopoe call across the mealies, you've heard my mother sing.

After supper it's time for the stories. Somehow, said Jafta, I think I almost love my mother best then—after the food and the hurrying, when the sun's going down and everything's quieter and cooler. Then she hugs us 'round her and chases away our sadness. We talk about today, and yesterday, and especially tomorrow.

Then, as the blanket of night spreads out over the world, with a bright moon above, my mother wraps us up carefully and with a kiss and goodnight puts us to sleep.

—Hugh Lewin

Happy he

With such a mother!

Faith in womankind

Beats with his blood.

—Alfred, Lord Tennyson

The Sound of My Name

Over and over
I call her back to me—
her flowered bathrobe
with pink trim around the collar
glasses a little crooked
hair wispy white.
Scuffing blue terrycloth slippers
she turns toward me,
grasping the counter edge for balance,
and speaks my name
with more love than anyone
ever squeezed into one word.
Over and over
I listen to the sound of my name—
the memory of her, speaking my name.

—Dilys Morris

Men are what their mothers made them.

—Emerson

My mother had a great deal of trouble
with me,
but I think she enjoyed it.

—Mark Twain

The best medicine in the world
is a mother's kiss.

—Anonymous

A mother is not a person to lean on
but a person to make leaning unnecessary.
—Dorothy Canfield Fisher

All that I am my mother made me.
—John Quincy Adams

What Your Mother Tells You Now

haha ga ima yu-koto
sono uchi ni
wakatte kuru

What your mother tells you now
in time
you will come to know.

—Mitsuye Yamada

Mama exhorted her children at every opportunity
to 'jump at de sun.'
We might not land on the sun,
but at least we would get off the ground.

—Zora Neale Hurston

Acknowledgments

Page 17, "Memories of Mama" by Annie S. Mitchell, a poem inspired by her mother, Sallie Bailey Schott. Copyright © 2004 by Annie S. Mitchell. Reprinted with permission from the author.

Page 24, "Baby Shoes" by Isla Paschal Richardson. Copyright © copyright Branden Publishing Company. Reprinted with permission.

Page 52-53, "Parents are People" written by Carol Hall. Copyright © by Free to Be Foundation, Inc.

Page 56-57, "Bundles of Joy" from *My Very Own Mother's Day* by Robin West. Copyright © 1996 by Carolrhoda Books, Inc., a division of Lerner Publishing Group. Used by permission of the publisher. All rights reserved.

Page 64-67, *Jafta's Mother* copyright © 1981. Written by Hugh Lewin, originally illustrated by Lisa Kopper.

Andrews McMeel Publishing has made every effort to contact the copyright holders.

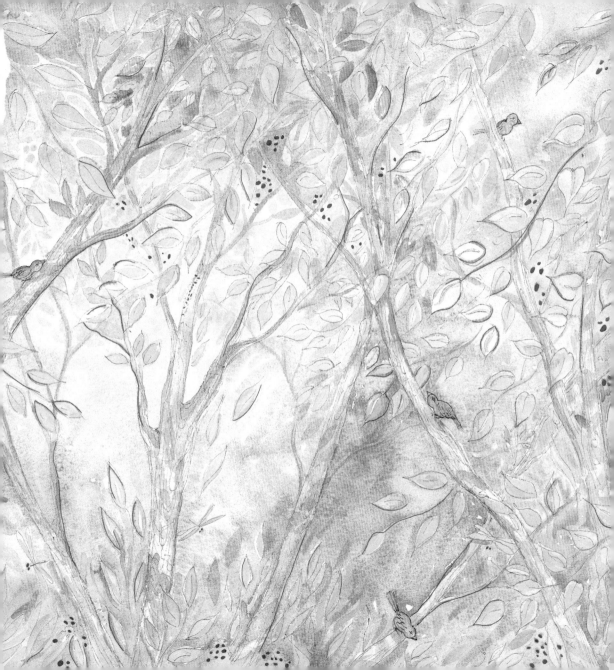

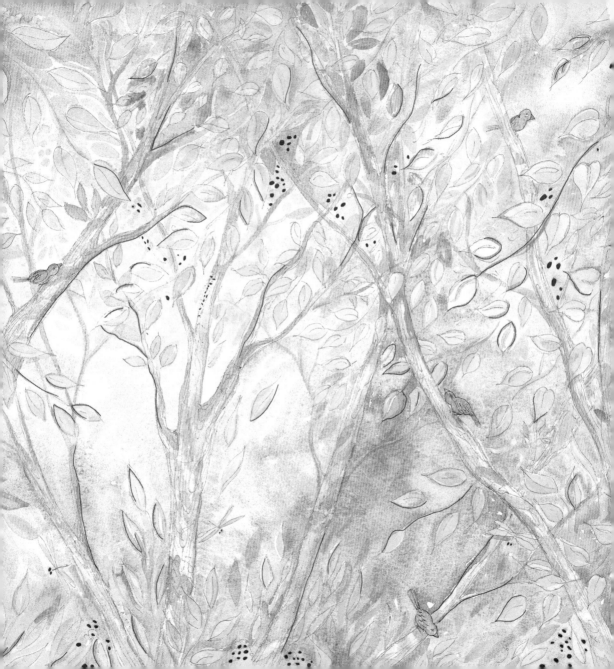